F.I.E.R.C.E:
The Awakening

Angelica Montgomery

KINGDOM LIFE PUBLISHING

ISBN: 9798537114420

DEDICATION

I would love to give honor and praise to my lord and savior Jesus the Christ. Secondly, to my beautiful family both immediate and extended, I love you all.

To all my spiritual children globally, I appreciate you all. It is an honor and humbling privilege to serve as your Apostle and leader.

CONTENTS

ACKNOWLEDGMENTS

I would like to acknowledge you, the reader! Thank you for taking the step to go deeper in God and invest in your spiritual understanding. Congratulations on your growth! I truly am excited about your future! More grace to you!

INTRODUCTION

It sometimes takes a while for us to experience moments in our life that make us feel far from God. We no longer can hear, feel, or have experiences as we normally would. We are left to believe that we can go no further or remain the same in our spirituality. It feels like we have been dropped and left on the sidelines. These times can come out of the blue or happen during a rough time in our life. I experienced these times right after seeking more in my relationship with God. I would spend hours crying out during intense worship. Often, we come across this during a highly spiritual service or an encounter during a conversation. We feel like God is standing right in front of us calling and embracing us. It happens through various experiences of our spiritual walk.

This is when we realize that God wants more for us. It makes us believe that there is more out there. He calls us to himself. He draws us to himself. Within ourselves this creates a hunger for more. So, we go seeking after him. The drawing and pulling can sometimes leave us feeling empty. Like there is something missing. Usually, this feeling happens within us all. One by one we go through these stages and sometimes misdiagnose it as depression. We do not even realize that it is and has been coined long ago as a "gift".

We typically verbalize or show this hunger. In conversations and how we live. Evidence is all around and under those tones of responding that we are fine. There is a sensitivity behind this feeling. People more in tune with what is going on in and around themselves can feel it. We can feel that we no longer can feel. To our knowledge we have "lost our way" to God.

Keep in mind that we are going to get back to God. There is just one more thing that we must address. Something that I believe does not get talked about quite often...Women. I believe that there is a season that we go through as women where we have given everything to God and worked things through except for the very things we have been told.

"Women are supposed to be seen and not heard."

"Women are barefoot and pregnant."

"Women should know their place."

What is our place? What do we really believe about ourselves? Do we know what God thinks about us?

These are important questions that I pray we answer in this book for you. It is important to understand that we are a part of God's master plan and purpose. Our contributions are necessary for the progression of the Kingdom of God.

Biblically we know this to be true because of the actions spreading of the gospel. You can argue that it is the women's need for importance and the urge to gossip. I believe the gospel was spread because of what the women had seen and experienced for themselves. Also, it is hardwired deep down in our DNA to want to improve our surroundings and culture.

The ongoing thought of protecting our young. Wanting better for them is also a driving force for changes to be made. Simply put, we do not want our children to have to endure the wrongs and hardships that we have experienced in our lives. It is also especially important for us to survive long enough to see our dreams and aspirations come true for ourselves.

When we see and know better, we want better. Depending on our character determines how we go about it. The compassion we have can cause something to set off inside of us to share what we know. If we have a personality that wants for itself then necessary moves will be made to get only that person ahead.

When women encounter something that we do not like or understand, we will ask questions and request input from others. I believe that society conditioning cannot control this from happening. This has proven to be true repeatedly throughout generations. In every walk of life. No matter how much we are told to "stay in our place", get married have lots of babies cause that's our "job". There is always an anomaly of a woman who will go against the normalities of society and do what everyone else has been thinking. I believe that God wanted it this way.

Eve's punishment after the garden of Eden was never meant to keep us in a box but just be the sentence written in our very make-up. Man ruling over women did not degrade her and make her property. Man was now even more responsible for what woman did. It reflected on him. I believe this is when man became the head. The statements before and after are my reasoning for these thoughts.

Genesis 3:16-17

"To the woman He said: "I will greatly multiply your sorrow and your conception; In pain you shall bring forth children; Your desire shall be for your husband, and he shall rule over you."

Then to Adam He said, "Because you have heeded the voice of your wife and have eaten from the tree of which I commanded you, saying, 'You shall not eat of it': "Cursed is the ground for your sake; In toil you shall eat of it All the days of your life.

Most people read this story in the Bible and destroy any hopes they have of women being used of God. This is added to another scripture that says women are saved in having children. We will discuss that one later. I never read the story that way and I hope I shared that point of view clearly. It is a clear pressure on my heart that we understand how many has evolved to making his sentence easier. We no longer must sweat and toil hard physically to gain access to food.

Why are we still struggling to advance in our thinking? So much has been restricted and confined. The ban on preciseness and poise is almost too much to deal with.

What is the standard now?

Who have we all become?

Can we answer those questions without losing the very defining fact, the standard of a God-Fearing Female Representation of Christ? We should all become God-fearing females living in excellence effectively.

God does want more from us women. He already died on the cross. He fulfilled the letter of the law so we could advance the kingdom. It is time to remove the hatred we secretly have in our heart towards ourselves. Women can evolve. We have already been redeemed. It can be extremely hard to achieve his desires and plans when there is so much that keeps you reflecting on what is more acceptable today.

To make things a little more relatable I will share some of my story to give you examples. It can be extremely hard to understand why things are happening even in your life and I can assure you that we all have those moments. We all have tests and trials. Going through things helps us to understand our purpose. We pick up tools and wisdom along our journey.

I want to make sure that you get a full understanding of why it is time to... Awaken!

CHAPTER 2

HERSTORY

I can recall many instances in our past that give definition to what women do when they want change. Some end in wars and riots others end with a beautiful change. More than often, it's been terrible when we don't think about the working parts of a matter. Throughout our history we have been given clues to how this happens. We tend to enter into terrible or rough times when we only look at one piece of the puzzle. I love history so; I will try not to include too many unnecessary facts.

One of the most dramatic and mismanaged, I believe is the events leading up to the Great Depression. I know that is what everyone was thinking. How? Beginning as far back as the 1800's and even earlier people were pouring into the US. They came from different cultures that treated drinking differently than what they were used to. Those same immigrants after drinking in the saloons and spending hard earned income on alcohol would beat and mistreat their families. This was unwelcomed in society. This was not the picture of the Country that those on the outside looking in wanted. Preachers and organizations lashed out for control of society and started to lobby for a ban on alcohol.

During these times women united and rose to start a union called Women's Christian Temperance Union. They marched down dirt road towns of their time and prayed right in front of saloons. This was an outrageous way for women to respond. They typically weren't even allowed in the saloons. Their behavior was strange, and it brought a spotlight on the issues. One older lady even went as far as literally tearing the club up in Kansas. She went from town to town smashing up saloons.

Soon they were facing an even bigger

problem. They forgot about home life. If anything, this is the way to get us even today. Tell us we are a bad mother or that we are neglecting our households and we go running back. We never want to be the bad seed of society or our children's childhood. Woman went back home leaving the torch to the Anti-Saloon League and another very infamous group.

While some states were making their own restrictions on alcohol, the goal was to amend it to the constitution. It took a while, but it finally happened. It went into effect causing the some of the greatest civil disobedience our nation had seen yet.

Everything changed when we crossed over from the teens. It brought the country into the roaring 20's. Woman's clothing and behavior in society took a turn. Our nation had just gone through a pandemic where friends and family had died. Now there was a ban on alcohol. There was a new outlook on life. Women dressed in shorter dresses & non-formed clothing. They were a different breed called flappers. They even drove themselves and of course there were more opportunities with technology after the war. More importantly everyone was now drinking men and women in public/private.

On paper it looked like the Prohibitionists had plenty of support. Almost immediately after the amendment was added just about everyone broke the law. There were many people that did not want this, and it led to some very tough times. Crime soared as speakeasies sprung up. Mobsters and gangsters fought over territory for the control of sales and corruption spread.

Following the infamous Valentine's day massacre everyone had enough of organized crime. Women step to the forefront again. This time they step in and protest to now do away with prohibition. Women's Organization for National Prohibition Reform is now on the other side calling for the legalization of alcohol. This time they petition on the steps of Congress. Eventually, they were able to make the changes they wanted to see.

Women want to contribute. Women want to live their own dreams. This was just one of the examples of evidence that it takes the contribution of women to assist in the growth of our society. This goes beyond the birthing of children.

Without women's contribution there would be no cause for the social life throughout history and our lives now. At the very least there is showing off. When someone has something better than the other person there is a desire to parade it down the street. How wealthy a man was seen by how well he took care of his family and "property". Could he provide was always in question.

The managerial skills and stewardship of

the women was also necessary. Men could not raise children on their own. Bringing in enough money to sustain the household was hard work enough. Society depended on the women to raise the children, maintain the household, and keep things in order so that the men could be left to their chores and their work. Afterwhile these duties were delegated to servants and maids. Men typically took care of the bookkeeping unless they hired a house manager or book/banker to tend to their financial requirements. After all, now there was income tax. A present to the government to help with all those dollars it would not receive for alcohol.

Throughout the years women began to

seek events and places for them to socialize throughout their day. Most of all the work was on the shoulders of housekeepers now so there was not much for the women to do. Unless you count picking the multiple courses for each meal of the day. Now enter sewing circles and visiting other ladies in the communities just in time for afternoon tea. Socializing events and parties of the decade would prove crucial to society. Women also evolved romantically and longed for companionship not just husbands. This would be a key tool in progressing in rank and status in society. Information circulated in communities because of the spreading of news due to technology such as the printed paper. Women set the tone for what was acceptable and decent.

What always proved steady and true was religion and even then, there was still a trinkle of women stepping to the forefront of stages and assemblies to the advancement of the Kingdom of God. You can call them missionaries. That is the title we typically give them in our local assemblies. Usually this begins with women gathering and spreading the gospel. Society was ok with these new sewing circles in most cases. It shows that they did not believe anything meaningful would come out of these meeting besides quilts, blankets, and new cycled gossip. If men were to gather and lead a secret movement it would threaten government and proven to be a dangerous threat, right? In history immediate and further back there is evidence continues of women taking a message or movement into their own hands to either make changes.

Another example of this is the women's rights movement for equality. Let us look at this for the sake of making clear my argument and not to promote it, ok. I do have some personal concerns about some things this movement stood for. This movement was making headway and gathering a lot of traction during the 1970's. The women had gone through many obstacles over the years. All efforts had gone through many approaches. Using various laws and taking their arguments to the highest court system. During a new attempt, was a new strategy. There was even an amendment presented that was going to be passed. They needed thirty-eight states to amend it into the Constitution. After a while all it would take is a few more signatures from states to adopt this new amendment and change our government concerning women. It was called the ERA (Equal Rights Amendment).

There was a ten-year window for the states needed to get on board and make the change for our society. Right before the deadline there was a push that no more states would join. Many televangelists jumped on this bandwagon to shut down any other state that would join in the revolution. It worked. The ERA fell short of the support it needed just by three states. The sad truth is that out of nowhere another force comes to the fore front to directly oppose what the other women were doing. Rallies would convince women of their views and that they did not want change. The claim was to be perfectly happy being completely reliant on their husband and to uphold the country's definition of what was a woman's place in society. Unfortunately, this movement was led down by another woman activist. She came out of nowhere. A housewife and mother of multiple (more than four) children. She was endorsed by many male leaders and now the voice of so many content household wives. It was surprising to see how she, being a submissive housewife, herself had taken to the big screen immediately. It was clear that those men wanted to make sure the opposing voice was a bit louder than those screaming for equality. Years of an agenda was overthrown because there was another woman on the other side.

To this day we still have the issues that was being fought for. I may not agree with everything. What I do know is that in my opinion there was a lack of compassion. Someone was unhappy with their life. To tell other people that they must deal with their cruel reality without any relief is terrible. At the foundation of our Christian belief is that we are to follow Christ. Jesus had compassion on those he performed miracles on. He meddled in just about every situation. Prostitution, the blind, the dumb, sinners, vile men, and such the like. If Jesus came to change people's lives for the better, then we should be in support of that. Just because it was not what she wanted we as woman still could have advanced had she joined in to make sure that certain aspects of her life were not changed. Not just for her sake but for those that would choose her lifestyle after her.

I remember when I first got married a lot of things was changing. One thing I am glad of is that I had enough sense to go and get a job for myself. Even with those victories and defeats of women before me nothing had changed about gender roles. My household growing up was different and right away Holy spirit had me pay attention to why there were certain issues in our homes. Simply put not everyone was raised around render roles. Some see their mothers do EVERYTHING. Some, like me, experience Daddy do all the housework.

I believe that it is because of this environment and the temperature of our culture, every generation of women are being tempted with change. Always looking to make a change.

CHAPTER 3

NOT FEMENISM

I believe that God wants us to evolve as human beings and learn from our mistakes. To learn from others. I believe that God chooses women because of our sensitive nature. It is sad to see so many denominations and churches discount women because of one scripture.

1 Timothy 2:11-15 reads as follows from the Amplified translation…

"A woman must quietly receive

instruction with all submissiveness. I do not allow a woman to teach or exercise authority over a man, but to remain quiet [in the congregation] For Adam was formed first [by God from the earth] then Eve, and it was not Adam who was deceived, but the woman who was led astray and fell into sin. But women will be preserved (saved) through [the pain and dangers of] the bearing of children if they continue in faith and love and holiness with self-control and discretion."

I do not agree that God wanted women to be silent. I do not believe that God wanted women to experience their new spiritual lives filtered through the eyes of their husbands. The reason being because there is only one scripture on women being silent in public. This same scripture talks about not usurping authority over men.

With this new formed following taking away so much from the traditional church, this Apostle, Paul did not want the women engaging publicly for societies sake. I know here we go again; however, it is important for us to know this. I believe that it became too much for the men of that day to handle. With the evolution and change of religion was as fragile as it is. I believe that it is like they just told the women to hold on we will get to you in a moment and just ended up silencing us for far too long.

We must make sure to know deep in our

minds and hearts that Apostle Paul was addressing an early church and there was a lot that was riding on the conversions. Gathering in a society of this day was an uprising and the fragile culture was monitored carefully by the church. Because of this the public appearance of women speaking was unheard of and possibly too much change for those days in Apostle Paul's eyes. After all this is the only time, we (women) are told to sit down and be quiet. Already the message of the ministry is controversial. Talking about changing people's lives with discussions on loving your enemy, raising the dead, performing the miraculous and delivering hope and good news to those that had no hope. I have a belief that because Paul was not around the original twelve perhaps, he did not see how much women contributed to the work of the ministry. He was thrown into this new life, literally blindsided. Also, in other books he mentions and has a high respect for women who worked in the ministry so it could just be the use of Paul's knowledge of local laws. I used to have a huge issue with this passage of scripture. It led me to believe that Apostle Paul had an issue with women. He probably did not see that he boasts about living a single lifestyle in the letters written to the church in Corinth.

1 Corinthians 7: 7-8,

> "I wish that all the people were as I am; but each person has his own gift

from God, one of this kind and one of that. But I say to the unmarried and to the widows, [that as a practical matter] it is good if they remain [single and entirely devoted to the Lord] as I am."

This allows us to believe that he was perfectly fine without a wife. He preferred it. He could do more for the work of the ministry because of celibacy and being single. This is wonderful for Apostle Paul. The truth is that was his gift, which he so neatly tells us. One of my gifts is that of marriage. Just like a gift we individually have to choose what we are going to do with it. It can be unused and thrown to the side. It can be opened and embraced. I had to choose to fulfill what was already placed in me. That is a part of another book Sleeping with the prophet. In truth these passages of scripture have been quoted so much and preached for so long that it has made it exceedingly difficult for women to advance in society.

Looking at our founding fathers of the United States of America you find that there were references made in our laws to the bible. Once again, not saying that we should be upset and ready to burn the whole thing down. I believe that to understand history and where we have already been prepares us for a future where we do not repeat history.

Over and over again we hear of how society has looked at women in high authority positions and literally thrown 1 Timothy 2:12 scripture at them. Yet, every generation and way of life all throughout history we see that there was always a woman who chose to deny society's roadblocks and cages. Something in those that went before us saw something that they wanted or did not want for themselves. They wanted better or they wanted change, so they asked questions and demanded answers and attention.

Eventually a woman would gain some ground. These fore mothers and trailblazers carved themselves up a nice small piece of the pie or they died in the middle of the fight. Things would quiet down, and women would be thrown back into the normal everyday humdrum of a life. Without our questions being answered and having to quietly live for generations we still have a growing hunger.

The definition of feminism is the doctrine advocating social, political, and all other rights of women equal to those of men. An organized movement for the attainment of such rights for women.

While the definition of feminism is important to understand, we must also remember that as Christian believers we cannot support any other doctrine other than that of Jesus Christ. The concern is that while pushing any movement other than the true Gospel will leave you on the outside of the real purpose God has for you. I rather have things work together for my good than for things to happen to others despite what

I considered to be good.

We should really look at feminism and how it holds up to the Bible. There is another scripture that I would like to point out it is something that makes everyone cringe.

Colossians 3:18, "Wives submit yourselves unto your own husbands as it is fit in the Lord."

Here we are getting to the foundation of women's constant rebellion. I believe that for centuries this was the one of the main scriptures that many women loathed. If anything, they wanted to live out their own lives and not marry. Each generation there were anomalous women that would hate to hear that they had to listen to authority. To listen to someone who they felt truly did not have their best interests at heart and only cared about their own desires, wants, and needs. There were many instances where young women would aspire to live out great lives and accomplish more things than just having children and being a housewife. This would cause many to go and live outside of societies norms. The thought was that whenever you were married you became property you became someone else's possession, and you are now a subject to another man. Schooling and lessons being centered around how you would please your husband and make proud the families that would take you in as a daughter-in-law.

How could it be that we are ready and

willing to create a world in which we submerged our daughters into a lifestyle of servitude. When it comes to salvation and serving God it is a struggle. To get the world and to surround ourselves with knowledge of how to please God. Becoming a new convert to believe in and be submerged into a lifestyle of deep relationship with God. This is just the conversation on marriage and the training that is put into making sure that man on earth is happy. We have not begun to discuss all the other institutions that are focused on the enjoyment of temporary things.

The interpretation of Colossians 3:18 is not necessarily aiming at controlling women. I believe that it was making sure women focus on their own husbands. Not to be more loyal to the authority and leadership of someone else's husband. In short, their own husband was being neglected. This looks like an issue that was widespread in the Church of the Colossians. Enough that it caused a lot of confusion and needed to be addressed in this passage. In all actuality it is still an issue today. Women are converted and become very zealous about their relationship with God, the church, and the ministry that they elevate their pastor or leader above the leadership of their own husband. They lost respect and consideration that they are living joined with another person and it is not just themselves submitted to an outside source.

We must understand that the doctrine of Jesus Christ is complete. There is nothing missing. Jesus has fulfilled all law and overcome all circumstances. His message gives us hope and brings us into a miraculous new life. No longer do we search for our own way or own ideas about how society should be. Once we come into alignment with everything that Jesus has showed us through the cross, baptism, repentance, and faith. We now have everything we need to fulfill the promise of greater works shall we do. We no longer get to sit back and wait for man to do what God ordained for us to do. He made us perfectly female, and we are to use everything he has put inside of us to do what he wants us to do. God has given us his spirit and his mind freely. We are now a part of a bigger plan and purpose when it comes to society. To fill what God has for us by remembering what he's done for us in doing what he's asked of us.

CHAPTER 4

BALANCED BIBLE

All over the Bible you can see where women contribute and are a part of their communities. Do not think that it is a coincidence that this is all throughout the bible. From cover to cover, start to finish we are given accounts of women being used and mentioned in the Bible. In all different walks of life there are countless examples of what it means to be used by God and to be a part of his purpose and plan.

Two of the main examples that I want to use are those that have their own books in the Bible. You have Ruth and Esther very key and important times that are presented through the eyes of women and their stories. God chooses to highlight these experiences to consider. If the plan were to be silent and to be quiet, there would never be these types of women even being mentioned in the Bible let alone given their own books. These women took a stand against what was the status quo of what was supposed to be followed. They decided it was far from acceptable to continue with how their lives were in their moment of greatest injustice. Standing in the gap, speaking out against traditions, being seen in higher courts, and against higher authorities so that they can live a better life and generations behind them can live and prosper.

The first book mentioned is Ruth. Her story is peculiar because it mentions two women majorly instead of just one. Ruth was not from Bethlehem, she was a Moabite woman married to Mahlon a son of Naomi, wife of Elimelech who had died.

Ruth 1:4-6,

> "they took wives from the Moabite women; the name of the one was Orpah, and the name of the other was Ruth. They lived there about ten years and then both Mahlon and Chilion also died, so the woman [Naomi] was left without her two sons and her

husband. Then she set out with her daughters-in-law to return from the country of Moab, for she had heard in Moab how the Lord had taken care of his people of Judah in giving them food."

Naomi took matters into her own hands. She no longer had a reason to remain in Moab. It would be perfectly safe among her own people. There was no need to stay in the position that they were with her husband and sons dead now who would provide until they died. Deciding that she would go back to the land in which she came from now that the famine was over there was no need for her to live in Moab. On the way she pleaded with her daughter in law to go back to the land which they came from and go back to their families. They needed husbands and they were able to remarry. Naomi did not want them to remain with her. She told them that she was the one dealt a hard blow (Ruth 1:13) There was no way to provide for both new husbands from sons she did not have. They refused, Orpah only once but Ruth was persistent and remained with Naomi.

This is not your typical story because of tradition and how things were done. When a spouse dies and especially when there are no children from that spouse, then you are free to marry again. These daughters-in-law were not even a part of the same culture. They were Moabites and had their own gods. Once getting to Bethlehem it is known that Naomi is back in town in that she has brought a foreigner back with her.

Ruth decides one day that she is going to go ahead and gleam from the fields harvesting barley and ended up in Boaz's (a next of kin) field. He acknowledges her and treats her with kindness all season long.

Seeing an opportunity for Naomi to give Ruth a husband which would be kindred she decided that they should not wait anymore for others to decide who gets the inheritance of Elimelech. This was normally something that the men would take up amongst themselves. It was taking them too long they got there at the beginning of the harvest, and it was now the end of the harvest how many times have we waited for other people to do what they should do in it takes entirely too long and it cost us too much time money in resources to do what they should have done all along we waste time energy our youth and God's agenda.

Naomi gives Ruth instructions that are far from traditional. To present herself in such a way that was not normal.

Ruth 3:14,

> "And she lay at his feet until the morning: and she rose up before one could know another. And he said, let it not be known that a woman came into the floor."

After all the instructions and spending the night in the threshing floor where all the

49

men were drunk and sleeping it was unheard of. Boaz still considered her reputation as virtuous woman. We will get to more of that a little later (wink). After the encounter Boaz had to take the matter to another next of kin who refused because his own inheritance was at stake. Ruth marries Boaz and gives birth to Obed the grandfather of David. Later becoming the great (times a whole lot) grandmothers of Jesus Christ. Ruth is also mentioned in the lineage of Jesus Christ in the book of Matthew.

Next, we have Queen Esther from her own book in the bible. Hadassah being her real name was a Jew. Her and her cousin Mordecai were in the land of their captivity so it was very tough for Jews at the time and so she had to conceal her identity. How many times do we as women have to be less than what we really are to appease those that are around us our communities our neighbors and onlookers?

Unfortunately, Esther story begins as another woman's story, Queen Vashti is ending. This vital part of the story is key to understand exactly the tension and the expectations of women back in those times. The very fact that Queen Vashti defied King Ahasuerus (A.K.A. Xerxes) openly at a weeklong party that he threw specifically to show off everything he owned to everyone. She refused to be a part of the parade. It made everyone so upset they demanded that something be done to correct this egregious act.

Esther 1:16-18

"Vashti the queen has not only wronged the king but [also] all the officials (royal representatives) and all the peoples who are in all the provinces of King Ahasuerus. For the queen's conduct will become known to all women, causing them to look on their husbands with contempt (disrespect) since they will say, 'King Ahasuerus commanded Queen Vashti to be brought before him, but she did not come'. This [very] day the ladies of Persia and Media who have heard of the queen's refusal will speak [in the same way] to all the king's officials, and there will be plenty of contempt and anger."

It probably would not have been so bad had Queen Vashti not been in a party herself that she had held for all the women. This was quite an audience to witness her disobedient, outlandish, and nontraditional behavior. The men around the king feared that all the women would be out of control and thus Queen Vashti was banished from the king's presence.

A law was put in place that began a search for a virgin to replace her. After a month-long process and grooming the King finally chose Esther, and she became Queen after Vashti.

What makes Esther's story so unique is that her posture was not because of selfish gain or boldness and defiance, rather than respect and obedience. Mordecai, a guardian cousin (who instructed her not to reveal her identity and heritage) warned her of two eunuchs that were plotting against the King. Esther gave the King the news and gave the credit to her cousin.

Later Mordecai encounters a man named Haman, the highest-ranking official in the government. The king had commanded that everyone honor him by bowing down and kneeling before him and Mordecai refused. A hatred for all the Jews led Haman to devise a plan to get rid of all the Jewish people. Once again Mordecai learned of the plot and warned Esther and pleaded with her to entreat the king. It took a lot of courage to defy a law that had just been put in place. She knew that she had to wait for the king to call her and here she was needing to go against that very law. She fasted for three days to see if her favor would be able to get the king to meet with her without being summoned or she would die. After the fast she had a plan of her own and found favor.

Ether 8:7

"Then King Ahasuerus said to Queen Esther and to Mordecai the Jew, "Behold I have given Esther the House of Haman, and they have hanged him on the gallows because he stretched out his hand against the Jews."

Although she was deafly afraid of what might happen, she knew that if she did nothing then all would be lost. Her contribution was so great. The stakes were no doubt high. She saved her fellow Jewish people from an untimely death.

Then there are the women who were apart of Jesus linage. One of my favorites was Tamar who was actually the daughter-in-law to Judah. She was taken as a wife to his son, Er who was evil in the sight of the Lord (Genesis 38:7) that God killed him. So, Onan was to go in and perform his duty to raise children in the name of his brother and he refused spilling his seed and God killed him. Of course, by now Judah clearly thought there was something wrong with Tamar and he sent her away to live with her father claiming that she could have the youngest son Sheila when he came of age. The fact being he had no real desire to give his youngest son to marry her because he thought that Shelah might die as well.

Tamar wore the proper widows clothing and went and lived with her father. Long enough after she saw that Sheila was grown and she had not been given to him. So, after learning that Judah's wife died and he was morning, she removed tradition and disguised herself sitting at the gates of where he was going waiting for Judah. Tamar realized that she would have to take matters into her own hands. Although she tricked

Judah into sleeping with her, Tamar would not be mishandled and treated as a broken mule. While the punishment for her crime was to be burned to death. She did not neglect secured her future and protected her honor in the process.

Genesis 38:25-26,

> "While she was being brought out, she [took the things Judah had given her and] sent [them along with a message] to her father-in-law, saying, "I am with child by the man to whom these articles belong." And she added. "Please examine [them carefully] and see [clearly] to whom these things belong, the seal and the core and staff."

Judah recognized the articles, and said, "She has been more righteous [in this matter] than I, because I did not give her to my son Shelah [as I had promised]." And Judah did not have [intimate] relations with her again."

She was also saved from a life of no meaning. Meaning that during a time when wife and motherhood was the ultimate goal, she could at least have one. Status was everything as well. Tamar gave birth and she blessed with twins Pharez and Zarah. Yes, that is the same Tamar and Pharez mentioned in the book of Matthew. Also, a part of the lineage of Jesus Christ.

All these examples show us that there is a purpose and a need for women's

59

contribution. We are supposed to come out of our comfort zones. When times get hard it can be easy to conform and do what has always been expected. When there is a higher purpose and reason outside of your immediate well-being, it takes a strong woman to know that something must be done. Many more women in the Bible had just that same opportunity to show that they could make a difference. They had to save their people or make memorable their family name. Women of the Bible moved out with courage and faith, knowing that what they were doing was not exactly right in their own eyes but was right for their time.

This would be the perfect time to let you know that we have covered a lot of ground so far during this book. It is important to understand that over the next few chapters we are going to deal with some heavy issues that we have had to endure at one point or another in our lives. The biggest one that we have talked about so being culture and societal restraints, not quiet in depth, I believe is the very that foundation we need. We are going to attack other areas and ally's where we have been caged and re-caged in the most. Are YOU ready?... let's continue.

CHAPTER 5

STUN: KEEP HER NUMB

Stun: to deprive of consciousness or strength by or as if by a blow, fall, etc. to astonish; astound; amaze: to shock; overwhelm: to cause astonishment or amazement: the act of stunning. the condition of being stunned.

Ministry began for me when I was fifteen years old. I was taught to teach bible study at an even younger age. We started at home and then there were special church gatherings and outreach ministry. I grew up singing as early as I could remember. Standing in front of crowds was something that I was not used to right away. Eventually, I learned to deal with the nervousness and the shaking when the power of God would come over me.

Preaching was a little different because I needed to speak. I had to prepare a message and make sure that it had substance. Some of my first audiences were not that of my peers but older saints in their twenties, thirties, forties, and up. I had to hold their attention. It was not easy but one thing I learned quickly was how to teach and give an understanding with little to no guidance of my own. That is not immensely popular nowadays.

This was a great start to a growing young woman. What else could you ask for as a teen? The biggest problem was that I had not experienced life yet.

Out of the seven who had graduated from high school children, only my sister (who was two years older than me) and myself remained in church. We had made a pact to stick it out together no matter what.

This is where I was dealt my own blow…It led me to make a choice (I made peace with it) to go to a school that was not on my list. Due to family deaths, it was necessary. My parents took it hard and there were physical side effects from the loss. It was a difficult time. Right during all that someone dear to the family died.

I thought that this was my Naomi moment my shock and awe, but it was only the beginning. There was one more death in the family that would leave a lasting effect on me. However, I was ready to lay down my plans and desires. I turned to prayer, fasting, and emerged myself into ministry. The places where my parents could not go, I would step in and be their replacement. I clearly had been stunned. This time it caused me to adjust with my plans.

Next, would go on to move in with my sister. These were difficult times for me and all the while I would still preach and teach throughout the city. There were even two ministries where I was a regular speaker, at least one to three times a month.

Amid all this life happening then I would meet and marry (because it happened quickly) my husband. I finally did something for myself, and it was not widely accepted. He was very well positioned and grown man of God. In other words, we were the same age, and he knew what he wanted. All those that I sacrificed my plans for strongly disapproved. So much so that we eloped. Now I was officially stunned overwhelmed by everything that had happened over the short period of time love me in a daze.

When we endure problem after problem, test after test, trial after trial, blow after blow and loss after loss it tends to leave us out of breath. it is the ultimate I can't breathe situation we're so much pressure is on us and were unable to move or even make the proper adjustments to get out from what's keeping us paralyzed. We are no longer aware and no longer able to participate in things that are going on around us. People believe that this is depression where you're not engaged, and you lose feeling, and you lose the ability to want to get up and do anything. One of the definitions of depression is the state of being sad and gloomy downcast pressed down lowered in force so it is true it's similar.

Being stunned reminds me of some of the documentaries that I've watched about lions' prides. The animals are so large and powerful that usually it takes multiple darts to take them out. So, depending on the strength and the capacity that you have, multiple darts and multiple situations will occur to make sure that you are stunned. No longer able to move because of the paralyzing pressure of the blows we have been dealt.

The purpose of making you unable to respond is so that when things happen (in society and on the outside of your life) you are unable to move. We will see what is happening but refuses to get involved. When things happen to other people and especially those who are less fortunate you will not help. You cannot help them get them out of a situation if you are bound yourself, right? If you are caged and have these overwhelming emotions and issues where it is one thing after another after another it will leave you worn out. What ministry? What encouragement? What exhortation? What can you do for others that you have not done for yourself?

However, being a part of the body of Christ and following the unction of Holy Spirit can shield others from the effects of us being stunned. Obedience and moving in what God tells us to do each time is necessary to getting out of this process. I was still preaching, and teaching while being stunned. The power of God was evident, and the people were still blessed, and I was stunned. I was working in ministry delivering the word of God laying on of

hands all the above and I was paralyzed.
He will often send us our very own form of
Ruth to help pull us out of our own personal
situations, administer the remedy.

Another side effects of being stunned, it
can also cause us to be very selfish and only
concerned about our immediate circle and
only those things that matter most to us
personally this happens with a lot of
believers who turn ineffective unable to
witness unable to win a soul to Christ unable
to save the lost because of their own selfish
motives due to paralyzing blows.

Isaiah 1:17,

"Learn to do good. Seek justice,
Rebuke the ruthless, Defend the
fatherless, Plead for the [rights of the]

widow [in court]."

"What you don't know can't hurt you." It would seem that secrets should shield us from being hurt. Hosea 4:6 tells us otherwise. When we are not aware that we have been hit and that there is a device being issued to take us out we can perish. It is like being frozen in time. Continuing out our days in a state where we are unable to grow unable to make a change and unable to care about our situation in the world around us. These seasons and moments happen to everyone.

We also will trust in corrupt systems. Pretending that everything is fine, and we do not need to get involved. Being in a state of shock causes irrational thinking. Leaving serious matters to people who are unqualified and have no sense of what justice is. They will abuse those that we have been commissioned to take care of. An injustice but justified.

What makes the difference is what you do wow being stunned and if you come out of being stunned.

It is important for us to remember that we are human and that things will happen out of our control. During this time I had a difficult time regaining my relationship with Christ. This will happen when we are brought to some type a feeling of being overwhelmed.

The word stun is a great explanation of what happened to me and what tends to happen right before someone has to deal with a downfall in their life. As for myself many of the things that I encountered disturbed me. It would be right before a struggle, and it seemed as though I would never recover from the shock.

CHAPTER 6

SUPPRESS: KEEP HER QUIET

Suppress: to put an end to the activities of (a person, body of persons, etc.) to do away with by or as by authority; abolish; stop (a practice, custom, etc.). to keep in or repress (a feeling, smile, groan, etc.) to withhold from disclosure or publication (truth, evidence, a book, names, etc.). to stop or arrest (a flow, hemorrhage, cough, etc.). to vanquish or subdue (a revolt, rebellion, etc.);

quell; crush.

There was so much that I was not even aware of until years later. More life was happening and soon it would go completely over the top. As, I found myself on the outs with God (so my family told me). It would take me a while to make amends and come face to face with the truth. That I had heard God's approval for myself. No one had to convince me. I did not know what my family wanted from me. What I did know was that allowing them to tell me what to do had kept me "in their good graces." Looking for their approval was almost equal to the opinion of God all those times before. That's where I lost my edge.

I lost all my confidence. If I had any left,

it was only to make sure that the chants and secret whispers of harmful wishes would never come true. It was obvious to me that I was on my own. In my family when a certain member stopped talking to one most of them would soon follow suit. The others would just be too busy to care or get involved.

It was very painful to be left out of some of the events. Thankfully, the summer was over by the time we really separated. However, that left two incredibly sad and lonely holidays. Thanksgiving and Christmas. They were spent that year with new traditions and new faces sitting across an assortment of different tables with strange dishes that I would have to learn to enjoy in some cases. Some situations were awkward, and others were a delight.

Many of us are never able to make it out of being stunned and therefore we fall into a suppression or what I like to also call silence. There is no movement. There is no engagement. There is only one emotion, anger. It is the equivalent of being zombie where we only feed on negative emotions and bitterness. Holding on to those things that we have experienced considering them the new normal and a part of our new surroundings.

We expect to be disappointed. So, we sit quiet in our darkness, and we expect to no longer be heard. This is what we are used to. It causes outbursts and frustration. We have become the brawling woman while trying not to be silent. Proverbs 21:9,25:24.

This is not the type of silence that is calm and delicate. It is the very example of the definition given at the beginning of this chapter. It puts an end to our activities. Does away with our confidence. Temporarily abolishes our faith in God. All the while keeping us crushed and withholding our voices from crying out for help. We repress our experiences, arresting our freedom from our shocking jolting traumas.

Remember a few chapters back when we talked about how women had made progress in a certain area? They were united as an organization and then suddenly most of the women disappeared. The pressure of the demands of our everyday life can also silence us. After trying to accomplish something great or simply going about your life are a dealt a terrible trial. We call ourselves trying to recover and we are met head on with expectations from our peers, and more important our families. This can cause us to second guess who we are and what we are supposed to be doing. I know that this is tough to talk about, but we have to many of us that are silent. Waiting on the next bake sale, PTA meeting and load of laundry and we do not want to talk because it seems exceedingly difficult. We already manage multiple people's lives. How can you manage your own life?

Now I know that some of you are super women, so I believe this one is for those that feel as if they are not satisfied with the efforts, they have been making. The way of life that we choose is to keep ourselves together, poised and in the elite of society. Overachieving is left to our children and husbands. The few that have maintained a slow growth while raising our families we tend to lose our footing having to restart in cycles. Pushing certain things to the back burner and leaving in the forefront those obvious things and issues that will get us the pat on the back that we deserve. The truth is that we are still dealing with society conditioning and the gender roles from the 1950s. It's not your husband's fault now, don't get upset at your spouse. The actual culprit holding you to these standards into this way of life is so much more complex. It's the fact that we hold these traditions to be higher and greater than the dreams and visions that God places in us. It is not to neglect on 1st works but to add to our lives into the good of the community.

The goal of the enemy for this season of our lives is to keep us quiet to keep us silent. Who better to quiet us than ourselves? It makes us feel as if there's something wrong with us and that we don't have the ability to make it out of our situation.

Many of us will continue to work businesses and participate in organizations while practicing being silent. Keeping our real   passions   and   desires   repressed. Choosing to be quelled we are ok with not being heard.

CHAPTER 7

SLEEP: KEEP HER DOWN

Sleep: to take the rest afforded by a suspension of voluntary bodily functions and the natural suspension, complete or partial, of consciousness; cease being awake.

It was an exceptionally low point of my life when I fell asleep when I no longer was conscious. Soon after I made a difficult decision for myself, I lost all support. What was even more hurtful was the fact that a decision not based on sin was considered out of the will of God. To those closest to me I was a lost cause. that took a turn into sleep. It felt like a nightmare. I lost a lot of confidence in the call on my life as well.

Everything that I was involved in and most of my ministry engagements was suddenly cancelled. Rumors of me backsliding when the truth was that I only got married started from the very ones who were close to me. Many people were upset. I did not owe them anything. The decision that had I made was for my future and I did not consult anyone who did not have my best future in mind. I sought the council of mentors and those that I looked up to. Everyone was confused because, I acted very quickly when God revealed what his will was it to me.

Unable to move. Unable to even grieve the loss of loved ones I was thrusted into a deep depression. I was now sleep. I lost the ability to influence all because people were so close to touch but out of reach. It would take deliverance to pull me out this one.

If we really spent hours and days praying and fasting for the answers that was given to us, how is it that were so easily depressed when someone else does not agree with us. All the confirmation and hearing the voice of God did not prepare me for this first blow. It was very devastating.

We can put others' opinions and expectations far above God's. especially when we have been searching for and what we have been praying for his will. To know that those that were close to us did not hear or feel the same thing. When the time comes that it does not it leaves us devastated.

All that ridicule sparked a hardness and a wall to go up around the depression. There is nothing worse than fortifying your depression with reasons and excuses "They wouldn't understand…" "No one has my best interest at heart anyways…" "I can hear God for myself, and I don't look up to them anyways…" everyone who was not a good example of a Godly woman was immediately disqualified from being a role model. Any mistake that they made we immediately write them off as a bad apple.

It is very evident that we have shut everyone off. Stop meeting with those that looked up to us. We believe deep down that no one can learn from us.

There is only one place where we feel more in control more alive more able to live with ourselves and what we have become. We throw ourselves into the role of housewife and mother. The responsibility of home life and the thought of keeping up with appearances weighs on us. We seek to be at peace in our home. If there is anything that we learned from a rough childhood is that home is the one place that you should feel comfortable and at rest. Jobs and families come in and take that away one at a time, so we have to figure out a way to reset our homes.

We focus on our ability to mother and to manage and to rule our small dwellings (no matter how many square feet it has) is our priority now. The responsibility that we placed on ourselves is heavy and can sometimes cost us our joy as it becomes a chore. There are times when we have a conversation that make us doubt that were even doing the bare minimum wrong.

We remember every conversation in detail that we've had about wanting a family. With our spouse or from a child to dream, to have a son. The pressure of having children is a happy distraction. We entertained the thought of bearing children and having a young one in our arms and being a loving mother. Being able to love a child is a beautiful thing. Whether you or someone else gave birth you are now the mother. To raise a child successfully is a triumph.

Life changes and soon we would shut down all together. It's a safe place for us. A great cover up. Throwing every reason to why we cannot do anything in ministry. The ultimate hiding excuse. Anything that we did not want to do got in the way of being wife and mother. It was overwhelming to do anything extra because we said so.

If we ever had experienced anything in God, it surely happened too long ago it is like those dreams that we have. They are so vivid almost as if it's a movie and yet overtime it slowly fades as we forget every detail. We experience life in these moments as if we are dreaming. there is no response mechanism our natural behaviors cease. we do not want to move because we cannot.

God can still speak to us. He allows an echo and repetition to continue during our slumber. You may think he has forgotten about you. I can assure you he has not. I know this to be true because of my own echo. Every so often occasionally I would see this thing, and it would remind me of where I came from and who I was. At first, I pretended to not know what it meant but it always caught my eye, and I would see it repeatedly wherever I was. God was there even when I was sleep.

Speaking of dreams. How fitting it is to talk about dreams when I mention being asleep. There are times when we dream that the picture is not clear; it can be fuzzy. It seems as if we are on the outside looking in. To some, it looks as if you are on the inside looking at the outside through a window on a rainy day. This is how we go through our day forcing caffeine and a pretending smile, watching everything happen around us without actually engaging ourselves. Moments where we would usually be passionate and very emotional instead are hard to connect to. It reminds me of when most of us as children go through being asleep for too long. Many of us can remember this issue or have experienced this. While sleeping, the dream we are having cuts randomly to a new scene. For example, we all of a sudden sit down on a toilet to use the bathroom. We immediately sense relief we feel lighter. Only to awake and soon realize that it was not a dream. What happened to us while we were dreaming was is an illusion. It was honestly the proper way to go about what was really happening to us. On another occasion while dreaming, I took a book to the bathroom with me and before I could sit down, I realized what was happening and woke myself up.

It is important for us to know that we must recognize that we're not feeling anymore. That we haven't really been passionate. When we don't really engage, we have to recognize and understand that we're not conscious and everything that makes us who we are has been suspended and no longer active. We are asleep.

CHAPTER 8

SIGNAL: WAKE HER UP

Signal: anything that serves to indicate, warn, direct, command, or the like, as a light, a gesture, an act, etc. anything agreed upon or understood as the occasion for concerted action. an act, event, or the like that causes or incites some action:

Only one month after my first child was born. He would have his very first sleep over. Afterwards I was told that it would become a regular event. What was I to do now? I did not want to negate my responsibilities. I was also hiding behind my duties. Honestly, I did not have anything to do without my child. Soon I found myself just waiting around for my husband to come home and my newborn child to come home.

There was no purpose other than to wait to steward others' lives. Wait to be needed. I was always there however this created another hole. This was my heart breaking. Another depth to the depression.

I had a new plan. I would venture into another form of ministry that I thought would be safer for me. It was busy work, and I exerted a lot of energy. I began dance ministry. The group was large, and I would not get any leads. Perfect. This was another cubby in the depression hole. Nothing disrupted.

I was thrusted in the spotlight because of my new husband's status. It was a tough thing to do because there was so much riding on appearances. The rejection from those who did not like that I was the one was tough for my new church home experience.

What made it worse was in the first years the parading and introductions of single young women by their mothers was evident. Like it was the social season all year long. It was hard to defend myself because I was sleep. I was timid and quiet. Not because I did not care. I could not respond. There was no energy or effort that I could muster up to even begin to defend myself.

Later I also joined the choir. It was another large group where I could be "used" and I could control just how much. Once again this was a mega church, and I was new. There would be no solos like what I did in my other churches. I could hide properly among this massive choir. Here I was now able to say that I was fully active in the ministry without having to be out front. Juggling the dance ministry, choir, and sometime helping in the café for breakfast was my new calling.

I speak a lot about when God calls you, it can be a continuous call until you pick up the phone. Mostly it is an echo from you going through your cycles. Each time I would complete a cycle and overcome things I would feel that pull into this and into that. I would often get signals and alarms. Like everyone I know. I would hit the snooze button.

As time went on, I began to feel comfortable with a few of the other young married women in the church around my age. It was refreshing to have friends again and to talk with someone while waiting for my husband to finish his duties as an armor bearer. While making these connections, the minister of music got married and I connected immediately to his new wife. She was genuinely nice and was I made a quick friend. The thing is there was something about her.

She did not waste any time starting a youth outreach program. I soon found myself sitting at a table and being invited to mentor young women at these events. See, this is the type of stuff that I was trying to avoid. It was very overwhelming. All the things that I went through came rushing back to me. I thought that I had left this behind. She was very convincing, and I gave in.

Here was the first alarm. I was a part of this type of ministry again. It would tug at me, and I would pull away. I pulled away so hard I put everything else in front of my obligations that I agreed to. Hitting the snooze button, I threw every excuse I could at what now was making me uncomfortable.

I now had three little children instead of one. I had to get a job and have a babysitter for my children. It was a remarkably busy schedule to keep. I still had to be active in the ministry. I did everything but that. I never showed up for one meeting.

After a wakeup call it would trigger and signal certain circumstances. For example, I had to start supporting my husband in ministry. We would drive around town going to various churches. After an exceedingly long day of stressful preparations, I was thrusted into ministry. My husband was preaching when there was a sudden flow of prophecy. As he began to minister to the young people, he yelled out my name. I handed one of my twins to a family member and joined him at the altar. I did not know what to expect. What began to happen was he asked me to work the altar with him. Out of nowhere like a ton of bricks I could feel again. Tears streamed down my face. How was this even possible. My tears had been reserved for angry prayers and frustration and here God was using me again to minister to others.

I believe this is to be considered a drawing out of sleep. When we are lulled awake. Not by an urge to use the bathroom. Think of your other senses. Like smelling bacon or coffee in the morning. This was another wake-up call and it works for a while but soon after I was in the between stage where we try to keep ourselves awake.

Even though we hear the alarm and get out of bed there are factors that can keep us from being fully awake. This time the outside sources are a huge determining factor. Not having anything to be passionate about can send you back to sleep. When there is nothing to engage in it can put you back in that slumber.

Many alarms are going off all around us. Some are screaming of God's love for us, some about the plans and joy that awaits. There are many things that God wants to give to us. He wants us to choose to be awake so he doesn't force us. We should desire to be in places that can keep us awake and not encourage us to snooze the alarm.

I have noticed that we will get another

jolt. We are pushed and rocked back and forth to startle us awake. A wake-up call that even when it comes to ministry and business, and we will look at it as if we need to hit snooze and say.

"Hey, don't wake me up I need five more minutes."

There are many times that we go to sleep, and we are in a deep dream then we wake up and do something crazy or a little too strange only to realize that we never woke up and we are still dreaming. There were many times that I have experienced this in the natural as well as in dream life.

When we get shaken awake its rough and moves our entire body. This wakes us up and makes us get going from whatever we were doing. Many people share in this unfortunate event. They are in a daze or deep dream, and they are playing a role they would never do if they were awake. We agree to sickness. Accept relationships that hurt our future. Allow others to make decisions that will hurt our relationship with God. When you're dreaming deeply you often ask for five more minutes to see where the dream goes. Best thing is that the alarm will ring again in just a little while.

CHAPTER 9

FIGHT OR FRIGHT

Fight- to engage in battle or in single combat; attempt to defend oneself against or to subdue, defeat, or destroy an adversary.to contend in any manner; strive vigorously for or against something. Fright- sudden and extreme fear; a sudden terror.

If there is anything that we should know, it is that this way of life (being a Christian) is not peaches and cream. There is a lot that we must endure to make sure that we are able to withstand every wile of the enemy.

We are not in a war because God wants things to be hard for us. We come into this knowing that destruction in our demise was the goal of our enemy before we came to Christ. Hopefully, I am not scaring you. The truth of the matter is many believe that the devil is a myth. You are already going to lose if you believe that there is nothing that you are fighting. (2 Corinthians 10: 3-5)

We are not God's children because we are weak but because we are strong. The idea that we take a vacation from life when we become saved is a grave error. We must fight for our freedom. We must fight to be awake.

There is a saying that says, "the grass is always greener on the other side". It talks about perception when you are in something versus looking in from the outside. The grass is greener on this side of salvation. You just must tend to it. Water and mow it. The grass is not greener on the other side where we came from. They are sadly mistaken. It is not. So, we must fight to remain in the kingdom of God.

Romans 8: 35-39 (AMP)

"who shall ever separate us from the love of Christ? Will tribulation, or distress, or persecution, or famine, or nakedness, or danger, or sword?

Just as it is written and forever remains

written,

"For your sake we are put to death all day long; We are regarded as sheep for the slaughter."

Yet in all these things we are more than conquerors and gain in overwhelming victory through him who loved us [so much that he died for us].

For I am convinced [and continued to be convinced-beyond any doubt] that neither death, nor life, nor angels, nor principalities, nor things present and threatening, nor things to come, nor powers, nor height, nor depth, nor any other created thing, will be able to separate us from the [unlimited] love of God, which is in Christ Jesus our Lord."

What has separated you? So far, we just mentioned life's events. Those outside circumstances that get in the way do not hold a candle to what will actually keep us from God. He gives us encouragement and dreams to give us an expected end. What do we do instead? We find ways to not do anything. We separate ourselves from any God aspirations. With the unsolicited assistance of fear.

With all the preparations and choosing and calling we now have to deal with those nasty f- words. They tell us that we will never be any good. Fear tells us that we are mediocre, and the bar is set too high. Fear gives no proof that any of these accusations are true. Before we even step out on what we know to be true here comes fear and then doubt who tag us and we give them premiere seating. A whole talk show in our minds. Entertaining fears, if we aren't careful, can suck us into a dark place. Back into being asleep.

We are brought out of darkness into his marvelous light. (1 Peter 2:9) When we have tests and trials come, it is not to take away but to add. With every new day and failed venture, It can feel as though we are being chipped away at. That everything that makes us is being stripped away until there is nothing left. This is God's way of making his light shine on every part of us. He does not want our flesh to hold us back. There can be no weakness anywhere inside. We should not be fearful of the battles that we will have to fight. God is with and in US.

Ultimately being afraid is a direct cause of the lack of faith. the reasons being that we have rejected what God has shown us about ourselves. Every time we hear good concerning ourselves, we speak negatively against it. We must be stretched in our faith. The only way to exercise something is to use it.

Hebrews 11:6

"But without faith it is impossible to please him: for he that cometh to God must believe that he is, and that he is a rewarder of them that diligently seek him.)

Our faith is important. What we believe in will make or break us. We really must replace our fear with faith. Pray for it and seek Him for it. God will love the fear out of you. It is like God answers our prayers like that excited and says…

"Ok, BET!" You want more of me!"

Breaking down that scripture and really think about what it is telling us would look like…

You cannot please God coming to him without the faith to believe that he is God.

You cannot please God without the faith to know that if you diligently seek him, he will not reward you.

It is not a game of hide and seek. God will let you win. You must look. Searching is the apart of the test. It is also a test of how much will you be able to stand. Do you have the endurance to at least come out of what's comfortable and search for him? We must earnestly want to win our search.

We have to understand that coming out of every stage will take a fight. There is no time to let up. When I was being pulled back into ministry it was difficult. Most days I didn't want to do it. I was afraid of what the people would say about it. After all they had condemned me to hell and here I was trying to Minister. I kept trying to shake shame. I kept trying to shake the feeling of being pulled. At least that would make the day to day better. I could hide in my parenting and wife duties. Everywhere I turned there was the pull. The draw. There was always a move of God. A reason to pray. A house full of young adults who wanted to be ministered too. Even while recalling all these events, I do not remember when I stopped going to the practices. When did I stop going to dance practice? I'm not sure. I do know that I slowly retreated in my mind from a lot of my obligations. The draw was too much to handle. These new responsibilities were too much. I had seen too much, encountered too much.

When we've decided that we are going to stay awake and see where these new surroundings and adventures take us we will slowly rise. We remove the things that held us down like a thin blanket. We will rub our eyes to make sure that we can see around us clearly. We stand up and take our stance to knock out whatever enemy would try to knock us back unconscious.

CHAPTER 10

AWAKENING

Awakening- rousing; quickening the act of awaking from sleep. a revival of interest or attention. a recognition, realization, or coming into awareness of something. a renewal of interest in religion, especially in a community; a revival.

When you have been awakened it is not an enlightenment without God. It is clearly another experience of who he is. He will ask you who are you then ask you who am I to you.

This is what we have been waiting for. With everything that has challenged us and created distance, now there's a clear path. An understanding and pull for us to open our eyes and live like we have never lived before.

There will be times when it might begin to feel as if yesterday was better. It is an illusion and not true. Each new day should be treated like another opportunity where must strategize. Praying for a revelation that will led us to a better tomorrow. Our deepened relationship with God will move us forward.

We have to let all the other temptations

and desires be irrelevant to us. Things may come to tell us that we should be normal and just like everyone else. They won't matter when push them aside. We have to cast down every imagination and idea that pretends to be greater than what we know is God.

Every conversation and those we hang around must be analyzed. We must put everyone in their proper compartment to make sure we are not tainted. It is a good practice to make sure that we surround ourselves with the people that speak the same. The only words we will hear from our friends are the same words of encouragement that were hear in our times of prayer. This is refusing to go back to sleep.

I remember accepting being fully awake at a conference. I had been given the opportunity to sing a solo. I had always sung in choirs and on praise teams, but this was different. It was the breaking point where I accepted that God was not finished with me yet. I no longer could deny what was on my life. I could no longer reject what God was calling me to do. There was a great peace that came over me after this encounter. My eyes were open, and I could see that all the issues I had endured up until this point did not compare to how God wanted to use me.

The truth about my awakening is that it came in spurts. It was like levels that I had to pass. Layers that had to be shed off me.

Being awake is a whole new atmosphere. Some of us have never experienced this. Its not the woke consciousness that has you boycott bad things or know a lot about a certain topic. This being awake means that you are aware.

You are now conscious all the passions and emotions and things that move you is no longer rooted in bitterness and anger. Now there's joy there's peace. Everything that once was dull and lack luster now has brightness to it a color there is welcoming enlightenment.

There is no plot that you are not aware of. All the enemies' devices and ways that he could possibly distract are known. This is just the beginning you are only coming into awareness. It is going to take a lot more to be fully stirred.

It is just like one of my favorite movies called the Matrix. Hopefully, you have already seen this movie. It was released in 1999. I do not want to spoil it for you so hopefully, you have.

The whole storyline consists of how there is a false world and a real world. There are people that are born and those that are grown in fields. The ones grown are in a vegetable state and are hooked up with multiple feeding and simulation tubes and cared for by the machines.

They only show one special person being "unplugged" the sound and movements of these mechanical tubes being unwind and removed from the flesh always makes me cringe. The fluid that is drained from the capsule-like housing resembles amniotic fluid and a womb.

The interesting thing is once all of the tubes have been removed, he is awake. Jolted by the sounds and pain all around him. The capsule-like housing once filled with fluid is drained and he is dumped out in a sewer. So now he is aware and in a weakened state. He is pulled out of the water to be taught and trained how to now live in a different world. Never to go back into that capsule.

We can all remain unplugged ourselves. There are plenty of things that we were doing and now we are slowly realizing that God wants us without all the things that so sloppily run and ruin our lives. Where we came from was an illusion of everything we will experience. A horrible dream where we could not respond.

There is an incredibly good reason why we should gain our full mobility. We will now be led to push the surroundings for other people to change. The best example of this comes in Ephesians 5:11-16 (AMP). Let us look at each verse.

[11] "Do not participate in the worthless *and* unproductive deeds of darkness, but instead expose them [by exemplifying personal integrity, moral

courage, and godly character];

[12] for it is disgraceful even to mention the things that such people practice in secret.

[13] But all things become visible when they are exposed by the light [of God's precepts], for [a]it is light that makes everything visible.

[14] For this reason He says,

"Awake, sleeper, And arise from the dead, And Christ will shine [as dawn] upon you *and* give you light."

[15] Therefore see that you walk carefully [living life with honor, purpose, and courage; shunning those who tolerate and enable evil], not as the unwise, but as wise [sensible, intelligent, discerning people],

[16] [b]making the very most of your time [on earth, recognizing and taking advantage of

each opportunity and using it with wisdom and diligence], because the days are [filled with] evil."

We are responsible for exposing deeds of darkness with our Godly ways. We are not to deal with darkness on its terms but God's way. The way we live will illuminate what was already in the light. Everything that we see around us doesn't have to be. Our living a life of God's purpose will outlive the actions of any darkness. God gives us light as we walk carefully. We must choose to make the most out of what he has given us.

It is not enough to be aware. We must take action.

Here is our opportunity and take a stand against those things that we see in our communities. We cannot be numb, refusing to act on what we see. The injustice, poverty, misrepresented, and those down and out. Everyone deserves a spokesperson.

This passage of scripture that we just read directly challenges us to be the hands and feet of Jesus Christ. We are not to sit still and wait for someone else to come along while we do not do what God has called us to do. He will quicken us. Pushing us to the edge waiting for us to take a leap. Our fight and faith without fear.

We have heard so much already and I know you have been reminded of every promise in every word. He got has not forgot so he is reminding you. There are empires in you the future is bright.

How can we ever go back after experiencing being awake? How can we want to no longer want freedom after knowing that we have been in a cage? You and I are now free! There is no reason to try and play like you do not know what's at stake. The first thing is you. Your future is at stake if you try to back to sleep. Be in love with living in the light. Awakening to Gods full purpose for you!

CHAPTER 11

GROWTH

If there is no opportunity for growth
where we have been converted it will feel
like something is missing. More than often,
it will be like a drought. We must progress
in our awakening. Completed development
is extremely important for effective
representation of Christ.

Once we are saved there comes a time
when we slowly lose our excitement.

Mostly due to life. The ups and downs. Disappointments and failure take their toll on us as we must figure out how to be saved and live a peaceful life.

We are missing a key component in our walk with God. Understanding. The lack of understanding is a huge issue in the body of Christ. There are a lot of places that do not teach about the tools needed to progress in our journey. Although there is some understanding of what is going on the fullness of the consequences is in a blind spot to unbelievers (John 6:44).

Right after salvation we have a feeling that all our problems go away, and we will find ourselves no longer going through anything. We walk out the door back to our homes and lives to find that we are the only thing that has changed, and life is now harder. Therefore, we lose people. They do not get the understanding and information that they need to progress in this life.

We never get informed that we have been awakened. We have been unplugged. We have come out of a state of being unaware. Oblivious is a better word.

Challenges come when we do not understand why we are going through tough times. Especially in a situation where those who have been awakened have not been taught how to seek the father. This can lead to being lazy. We are sent into a position where we expect everything to be done for us. It can be quite easy to get stuck doing the bare minimum in this case. Not because we believe that is what God wants from us but because its comfortable.

We are used to the convenient and readily accessible. We will even get really close to God. Praying, for him to use us. then he tests us with the answer. It will feel like we are going through the biggest valley. Sometimes, he will get quiet. In most cases people will back up and run the opposite direction when this happens. Why because they fail the test. We say we want more. God wants us to seek him. (Isaiah 55:6)

If everything we needed to succeed were readily accessible, everyone would immediately be fully capable. When we first get saved, we would be fully trained. We would have all the knowledge required to operate in every gift and ability. Not so. We must grow in this. Be stretched. We must exercise our gift to gain the capacity for what God wants us to know and do. In every way, being awaken to the plan God has for us will make us responsible to those around us and for those coming up behind us. In many cases we will find ourselves revolutionizing some aspect of our immediate society. We must be ready to stand out front and not retreat. You are the person the world has been waiting on.

Romans 8:19,

> "For the earnest expectation of the creature waiteth for the manifestation

of the sons of God."

You cannot go back to the way things were yesterday. Any experiences that you have had will not compare to walking in this fullness. You are whole rejoined to Christ fully.

It is not his will that we return to our old ways because we feel as though God has left us or that we no longer are a Christian because we do not feel God. Let us grow past this and move past this stage that so many of us get caught up in. (Hebrews 5:11-14) We are God's sons. Yes, even us women are sons. We receive an inheritance in the kingdom of God. We are responsible for people, vineyards, and talents. This is a good starting point for training. Identity.

As women we can get stuck in the middle of being awake and being active. There are so many things that poses a threat to us if we are active. There must be training to ensure that once we get going there is nothing that will stop us and anything in our way is prey for us to take down. I like to take our cue from that same lion's pride. For the growth of their pride, larger animals and faster animals must be taken down. The Lionesses come together with one goal…to provide for their pride.

Jude 1:20-23 (AMP),

"But you, beloved, build yourselves up on [the foundation of] your most holy faith [continually progress, rise like an edifice higher and higher], pray in the Holy Spirit, 21 and keep yourselves in the love of God, waiting anxiously and looking forward to the mercy of our Lord Jesus Christ [which will bring you] to eternal life. 22 And have mercy on some, who are doubting; 23 save others, snatching them out of the fire; and on some have mercy but with fear, loathing even the clothing spotted and polluted by their shameless immoral freedom."

This is a good example of what we who are new to awakening should do. It is more than being encouraged to come to church and to get involved in ministry. This education goes beyond that. We are to follow these instructions across the board. Scriptures like this are not reserved to the seasoned saints but to everyone. If you are now alive in Christ, it is time for you to grow a little more.

I have been a part of several churches where there was a very brief instruction time. A certificate of completion was given then you were thrown into ministry. I understand this is a good idea. It more so makes everything equal and the same. It does not leave any room for someone to be dropped. That is what we think happens. Unfortunately, most fly under the radar and become confused about the very basics of ministry. Beyond that is an even greater issue. Life. All the problems and trials can get to us. Especially when we have not learned how to apply what we have learned. It is easy to go back and desire what was once "easier" as they say. Those everyday obligations can still tempt us to go back to the way things were. We should hold on to the new relationship that we have in Jesus.

This is not about who has the best and biggest relationship with God. We understand that when the disciples argued over who would be the greatest in God's kingdom. (Matthew 18, Luke 9). We have to keep in mind that our salvation is just that and we must always be building ourselves.

This type of awareness. This can often be too much for most people to bear. Why? It will often lead to a jolt of energy. They are excited and extremely passionate. Most feel as though nothing is impossible. So, God once again tests them on that belief. If they have not been prepared for a long race, then those same ones can get burned out. All because there is no more fire left to keep going. This can happen to leaders and those new to salvation. There are no determining factors that tell us what level of our salvation that we will be in when we are awake.

One thing that is for sure is that there is always more room for growth. We should grow in an awareness of everything about the Kingdom of God. Building the understanding and knowledge well so that we aren't so easily defeated. We cannot afford, as the body of Christ to lose anyone's contribution because there was no one to teach or train.

CHAPTER 12

RESPONSIBILITY

We have been awakened and our path is clearer than ever. All the questions of why I am here, and what I am supposed to be doing are answered. It is important when our purpose is unlocked that we do not forget the foundation it was given. The very tests and trials that we went through to get where we are. Not forgetting that we needed so much guidance and prayer ourselves.

We are still defeating the status quo. Defying every normal behavior that is imposed on us as women. We no longer are angry but passionate and professional. We do not gossip but only speak about love with truth and facts. Our meetings and gatherings are impactful and causes others to join in and rethink how they live their lives.

Being measured by our ability to get married and have children is history now. The standard is to be successful in other areas of our lives. We have been given the ability to have a good career or job. There are many other hats that we must wear. If we want to take off a hat we hire and train someone else to do it. what shocked me was that this was biblical. Women could be as successful as we wanted to, and it would benefit society. This is what the stories in the bible of women encourage us to do. When we get caught up in only our tiny circle it can be restricting. Our freedom is reached when we act outside of our boxes like the women in the bible. It should inspire us to be more responsible for the world around us.

When I discovered the Proverbs 31-woman description it was the beginning of a shift in me. I was fourteen years old when I first read this passage of scripture. I did women's events and heard it quoted many times. Everywhere you turned women were having some form of "far above rubies" gathering. The point of these meetings was that we were to be like her so that we could keep our families proud. If you did not have a family somehow it showed what you were to be like if you did get married so that you would know what was expected of you. Only a virtuous woman would be sought after for marriage. We saw that once again marriage status and children as success in modern day ministry. And it very well should be a trophy for having children. There should be a trophy for raising children. This should not measure our worth as women.

Thank God for a revelation that took more than seven plus years later to finally receive the revelation behind it. It was not a scripture just about what made this woman more valuable than others. In fact, the Proverbs 31 woman was a mogul of her time. She broke through every normal behavior that we had been taught. Her ability to do so this and that was the virtuous part of her life. I knew that this was what God wanted for women all around. He wants us to be modern day Proverbs 31 women. Because she was a fruitful woman everyone else could be. We can represent Christ the best way that we know how. We can now step into powerful positions because we have scriptural backing.

Being a woman in a position of authority in a workplace has gotten better. It is quite different from ministry and workplace. In the workplace there is no one looking for you to have a husband or even looking for a man to say the same things that you are saying. They do not look over your shoulder to see if there is a male figure nodding in approval. When you are training someone it is agreed that you have been put in that position because you already know everything about that subject, and you practice it to the liking of those over you.

When you are in some type of authority in ministry it can be difficult. You still need constant reassuring from those above you. It makes it so much better when that person is a male. I have noticed that when I would make a statement even if it were sparked or prompted by holy spirit that it would be challenged. I wondered why there was so many questions when I would speak. I chopped this up to sexism and ignored the person from that time on. They would cause me to question everything that I knew. It was an exceedingly difficult process to go thru. I finally had to get things together so that I would be able to be an example for Christ. It took me a long time to be ok and comfortable to be questioned on whatever I was teaching at that time.

I had to be able to endure difficult

students. People who needed to be trained out of only looking for males to be the standard for the Kingdom of God. The truth was I had the knowledge I knew and could give so much to others. I had to get that off me and it came by way of a deliverance one day. Even leaders need to be quipped for the responsibility. The truth is if you are bound by a skewed perception, it can be on you. Like a cloak around your mind clouding your thoughts and viewpoint. You cannot see anything past the cloud.

If we do not navigate around what sets us back, we will lose others. Looking at everyone thinking that they are underestimating you will cancel any progress you ever have or will make. Until we keep our eyes and minds focused on what the issues really are we will fail.

The biggest tests that we will go through after moving in our calling is to see if we can share information. Everyone should be able to train other people. Being a Christian is not a normal way of life. Holy spirit shows us all truth. We should want what we have started to continue long after we have died.

The biggest fail of our life would be to die with nothing left behind. You may get a week or a month for everyone to remember you. The funeral would be short or long. There will be tears and heartfelt condolences to your family. What will be left of your legacy How will we ever know that you made progress in our communities. There must be a visible legacy. Conferences will end and ministry engagements will cease. Those long business meetings and conventions will slow down. What matters is if someone will carry on what you have started. We cannot be afraid of what we start if it would change. It should evolve itself for the needs of the day.

It reminds me of song artists. Some of their music grow old with us. They make albums throughout the decades. Some only lasts for a few years. They are often called one hit wonders. When we do not expect to be a generational solution, anything we do will die with us. Even the people that we remember on certain holidays contributed generationally.

It is your responsibility to train others. If you see someone struggling to do what you have achieved offer to be a mentor. We must not be such sorry losers that we think everything is a competition. There are way too many people in the world. We should reach back and grab those coming up behind us. You never know who would want to help you.

Do not lose faith on the assignment that God has given you. He is not going to take it back and no one can take it away from you. You have inside of you something that cannot be copied so remember to train and bring up others so they can be equipped for what's inside of them.

FOR BOOKS, SPEAKING ENGAGEMENTS, AND INTERVIEWS

angelicainternational@gmail.com

www.fiercetakeover.com